Manifesting
The Law of Attraction and You

I0159592

Manifesting
The Law of Attraction and You

The secret to creating the life you want by using the
Law of Attraction to manifest miracles

K.C Thomas

What The...?!? Publishing

Copyright/Disclaimer

Contents

CHAPTER 1

INTRODUCTION

And Jesus said to him, "'If you can?' All things are possible to him who believes." Mark 9:23

Imagine...

You wake up gently as the sunlight creeps across the bed, slowly drifting across your eyes. As you become aware of your surroundings, you glance over at your partner, remembering how amazing and lucky you were to find them. As you start waking up more fully, you rise out of bed, taking your time because you're not in a rush to get to work.

As you make your way to the kitchen, you reflect back on how your life was years ago before you discovered an important universal law of nature that you gradually learned how to take advantage of. Making breakfast for you and your partner, you reflect on how much had changed since that fated day.

Before, you used to struggle to make ends meet, working at a job you hated, only to look forward to coming back to where you stayed (could never bring yourself to call it home because of the run down apartment you could barely afford to rent on the bad side of town), you remembered how lonely and angry you felt all the time. You were so frustrated because you felt you weren't living the life you were meant to live.

That was before you discovered something important. You weren't sure where you first heard about it. Maybe you had been watching a talk show and heard someone mention it, or maybe it was a friend or colleague that talked about it casually at the water cooler, but slowly you became aware of the buzz surrounding something called The Law of Attraction. After hearing about it a few times, you decided to find out more about it. What you learned in your research created a burning desire to learn more. It was this desire that led you to this point in your life today.

Money was no longer a struggle, you have someone who you love deeply, and who loves you just as much. You make a living doing what you love and get to work with people who bring joy to your life. You just wish more people took the Law of Attraction more seriously. If they did, they could have everything they ever wanted as well...

Does this sound like a fantasy, or maybe a new Hallmark® movie? Surprisingly enough, more and more people are learning that it isn't a dream, that if they apply this law in their life, over time, they too start living the life they felt they were destined to live. The information has been around for thousands of years, but has only recently became more accessible thanks in part to the internet and books like The Secret.

But they only tell part of the story. In a perfect world, it would work exactly as advertised. Unfortunately, this isn't a perfect world. We do a lot to sabotage ourselves, either knowingly or unknowingly, and it's the main reason people feel hopeless and unable to pull themselves out of the rut they're currently stuck in.

I'll be honest, it's not always an easy process implement the Law of Attraction into your life because of preconceived notions or deeply held beliefs, but once you do, and really believe it can help you, then the life you were meant to live will begin to manifest itself around you.

CHAPTER 2

THE PROCESS

The basic process for activating the Law of Attraction is pretty straight forward. The actual steps you go through could easily be accomplished in a few minutes once you get the hang of it. All it really requires is a clear idea of what you want to accomplish and some time to focus on the results. It's the subtle stuff that makes the results so variable.

What I mean is, what your thoughts are, what you say to yourself, can have a huge impact on the results you see when trying to use the Law of Attraction to manifest something in your life. We'll go into the possible hangups you might run into in chapter 5, but honestly, the cause of most problems has more to do with your inner environment and thought processes than anything "out there."

With that said, the next section will go over the basic steps needed to start the manifestation process.

The Basic Steps

The stripped down process is:

1. Determine what you want the outcome to be

2. Frame your outcome in positive language

3. Determine if there's anything mentally or emotionally that might be at odds with your desired outcome.

4.   If at all possible, try to come up with a visual representation of your desired outcome

5.   Find a quiet place to focus on your desired outcome

6.   Take Action

More In-Depth review of the steps

Doesn't sound too challenging, does it? Surprisingly, there's a lot more going on than what's apparent on the surface. Each step has a lot going on in the background. So next up, I'm going to go into more depth for each step.

Step 1 - Determine what outcome you want

Of all the steps, this one is arguably the most important. Surprisingly, this is the step people have the most difficulty with. What people think they want usually isn't what they actually want.

As surprising as this sounds, it's pretty common. The biggest issue is that people focus more on what they don't want in the mistaken belief that they're focusing on what they really want. For example, say you have a vehicle that breaks down a lot.

What you want is: a reliable vehicle, or quite possibly a new vehicle. What actually happens is: you focus on your vehicle breaking down all the time. I'll cover this more in step 3, but what it really comes down to is focusing on the current negative situation instead of focusing on the desired, positive outcome.

The other possibility is that you think you know what you want, but there might be a much better outcome that you're overlooking.

An example of this would be when you don't like the people you work with. You might believe that what you want is for everyone to treat you better. Or maybe you hope they'll quit so someone new would take their place.

While you might think that's the perfect outcome, what might actually be better is to find a new job. With a new job, you would be surround by new people, new opportunities to advance, possibly better pay, along with a whole host of other possible bonuses. So while you might focus on changing your current environment, what you really want deep down is a complete change of environment.

With all that said, for this step, take some time to actually consider what you truly want. Don't just create a half formed, spur of the moment type desire. Really consider what it is you want while leaving yourself open to something better. Your unconscious, higher self knows what's best for you, but it can only act if you let it. Which brings us to the next step.

Step 2 - Framing your outcome in positive language

Most people, when they first learn about the Law of Attraction and manifesting, create outcomes that are at odds with what they really want. They don't realize they've done it, but at the end of the day, instead of attracting what they want, they wind up attracting more of what they don't want because of the language they use to craft their request. This is one of the main reasons the critics state that manifesting doesn't work.

It all boils down to the language your subconscious mind recognizes and uses to process information. Almost without exception, your subconscious mind ignores negative language. For example, if your desire is, "I don't want my car to break down," what your subconscious mind really hears is, "I want my car to break down."

Sure, with enough effort and proper visualization, you could get the, "I don't want my car to break down," request to work, but it would really be a case of your visualization overpowering the verbal component of your request.

The real question is, why would you want to struggle that much? Wouldn't it be much simpler, and easier, to just rephrase the request to become, "I want my car to run smoothly and reliably?" With that slight modification, you make it easy to match your visualizations with your words... your desire to your intentions. Instead of trying to swim upstream, you go with the flow down-stream.

Once you have a solid idea of what you actually want your outcome to be, you move on to the next step.

Step 3 - What might be blocking you?

This is the second biggest area people have problems with when it comes to implementing the Law of Attraction. In a lot of ways, it can be argued to actually be the hardest step to address, mainly because a lot of the resistance you'll face is buried in your subconscious. If you're not consciously aware of it, how do you change it?

The simple answer is, you can't... at least not directly. The more complicated answer is, you have to be observant of your thought processes and what you repeatedly tell yourself. By doing this, you can start to notice certain patterns of thought that you need to clear out in order to move forward with your manifesting goals. I'll go more into how to clear out blockages in chapter 4, but suffice it to say, if you can identify it, you can clear it. If you can't identify it, then you can do a general clearing processes that, while taking a lot longer to progress through, can eventually clear out blockages indirectly.

A good example of a blockage that most people suffer from, to some degree, revolves around money. Love it or hate it, most people have hang-ups when it comes to money and earning it. While you consciously say you want to make more money, for example, you might unconsciously believe that money is "the root of all evil." Or maybe your parents might have impressed upon you that, "money doesn't grow on trees," or that rich people were bad/selfish/evil/greedy/negative. The funny thing is, these 'evil' people seem to always be the ones who are making significantly more than your parents, never the same or less.

People have a tendency to think that whatever level of income they have is fine, it's only those 'greedy' people who make/have more money that are evil. If they somehow find a way to start making more money, however, then suddenly that new, higher amount of income is fine, but those people who still make more than their new level of income are the 'bad people.'

If you were exposed to these types of thoughts/ideas from a young age (you likely were), from people you love and trusted (because they didn't know any better), then these beliefs probably became ingrained in your subconscious mind. Because of this, you might think, "I want to make more money, but not too much because I don't want to be greedy." Unfortunately, that sends a message to your unconscious mind to not let you make any significant improvement in your financial life. You might make a bit more money, but nothing earth-shattering. More likely though, you'll get that raise or get a new job where you make more, but a monthly bill or something similar will raise its ugly head, or something will break down/need to be replaced, that limits your effect income to remain at about the same level.

Until you clear out that belief that money is somehow bad or wrong, you're going to be stuck spinning your wheels, eventually giving up and saying that the Law of Attraction doesn't work, or best case scenario, that it just doesn't work for you. The fact of the matter is, it works for everyone. It's just a matter of taking your foot off the brake when you put your foot on the gas.

The good news is, not every goal/desire you have will have such a deep-seated block. For a lot of things, you might not encounter any resistance at all. In those cases, you might be shocked by how fast you can manifest something. There's been times where I've done tiny tests, things that might be coincidental, but highly unlikely, to test out the process. Thinks like seeing a coffee cup with a specific design on it (took me 2 days to manifest that outcome), or getting a parking spot close to the entrance (9 time out of 10 I get within ten car slots away from the door).

Since I don't have any strongly held beliefs that keep me from thinking it's unusual to find a parking spot close to the door, I have a very high success ratio in finding them. The same is true when it comes to finding spare change on the ground. Once I focus my attention on it, I seem to start finding change all over the place. I've been able to find enough in one day to buy a soda when I was thirsty and had forgotten to bring any cash with me.

What this all boils down to is, if you have a desire to manifest something and it seems to be taking a long time to arrive, you might have some clearing to do in order for it to arrive faster.

Step 4 - Creating a visual representation

The next step in the process, assuming you've done a good job of really determining what you want, is developing a visualization, and a matching affirmation, for your desire. If you want a new car, then it's not good enough to just say, "I want a new car." That type of request carries very little power with it. The more specific you can become with your visualization, the more energy you invest in it.

It comes back to the fact that it's going to be your subconscious mind that powers the manifestation process. Your subconscious only reacts mildly to verbal cues. Don't get me wrong, doing things like repeating affirmations will have a big, positive affect on your results, but the real workhorse is having a mental representation of what you're trying to manifest.

The reason this is so important is because your subconscious mind works in pictures and images, not words. When you repeat an affirmation to yourself, unless you've consciously created a visualization beforehand, your subconscious mind is going to spontaneously generate a visualization for the words. Because the visualization is basically random and subject to change every time you do it, it only holds a little power.

On the other hand, if you develop a strong mental image of what you want, continuing the previous example: the make, model, color, and any shiny bits of the exact vehicle you want, your subconscious is going to latch on to it. From there, after a few repetitions, every time you repeat your affirmation, your subconscious mind is going to recreate that image. It's also going to strengthen the visualization, making it even easier to see it in your mind after every repetition. Just like a snowball rolling downhill, it picks up speed and momentum, until eventually it becomes an unstoppable force.

At that point, it becomes a matter of when, not if, you'll manifest your desire. There is a caveat to this idea about when it'll show up. I'll touch on it more in chapter 4, but the fact of the matter is, even if you do all the steps perfectly, your subconscious mind always has your best interest at heart and will try any bring your desire to fruition, when possible, but sometimes it might delay its arrival in order to let something even better happen.

For example, while you might desire a raise at work, your subconscious mind might delay you from getting it so you'll take, and finish, a night class that'll let you have a chance encounter with someone who knows someone who is looking for a person with your skills and talents, someone who'll hire you at a significantly higher salary. If your subconscious had simply manifested a raise at your current job, you might not have been inclined to take the night class, thereby causing you to miss the better opportunity. So not getting what you wished for might actually be the best thing for you.

Another thing you need to do is add as much emotional content to the visualization as possible. The reason you work so hard to create a mental image of what you want is to stir up your emotions, which is the fuel needed to really supercharge your desire for attracting it. Your emotions are the raw power that fuels the manifestation, being concentrated like a magnifying lens through your mental image, and brought into focus by your affirmations.

Step 5 - Finding a quiet place to focus on your outcome

Once you have the previous four steps out of the way, the next step is where the magic starts to happen. Everything up to this point has just been the preparatory work.

For almost every attempt you make to manifest your heart's desire, you'll need to intensely focus on what you want; to actually work at visualizing your desire to allow it to manifest in the physical world. While you might be one of those rare individuals that can do this process anywhere, or you've gotten so comfortable with the process that it flows easily, to get the most benefit/results, you'll want to find a quiet spot to go through this process, someplace with minimal or no distractions.

This might be as simple as going to a specific room in your house, possibly hanging a sign on the door that you don't want to be disturbed. If you find it difficult to concentrate in a completely quiet environment, or there's noise in the background that's distracting, playing soft classical music or something similar, something that doesn't have spoken words would be appropriate. In the next chapter I'll go into other audio options that might improve your results. For now though, you just want an environment that's conducive to quiet contemplation of your desire.

Getting yourself in a comfortable position, either sitting or lying down, you'll want to go through a process of relaxing yourself before you start focusing on your request. If you're stressed or tense, you're going to block your subconscious mind from being able start working on your request. So once you're fully relaxed, you're going to start concentrating on your visualization while softly repeating your affirmation.

The goal isn't to do it in a bored fashion, but in a highly focused manner. With that in mind, don't draw this session out so long that you start to wander in your thoughts. If that happens, you'll give your subconscious mind the idea that you're really not that interested in whatever you desire, so it's not going to work hard to manifest it. It's better to have a very short and sweet session where you're able to invest a lot of emotion and energy to rath-

15

er than a long, drawn out session that leaves you rung out at the end. This is another reason you want to give your visualization an emotional charge, to help keep you focused on the end result.

At this point, there's two different schools of thought on this process. One school is, once you've done this process once, you should let it go and never revisit it until your desire manifests itself. The other school advises doing this process on a regular basis until it shows up.

The reasoning behind the one shot method is the belief that, if you keep repeating your request to your subconscious, you'll give it the impression that you don't really believe it can create it physically, thereby weakening the manifestation.

The other side of the argument is, people who advocate you do this process regularly have the belief that, due to the repetition, you make it seem real in your life, like it's already here for you to enjoy and you just have to find it. I also personally think that the repetition helps it get to your subconscious mind more effectively, at least at the beginning of your journey.

For most people, it will take time for you to develop that bridge of trust and communication with your subconscious mind, so the initial repetition is there to let your subconscious know that you really are, in fact, trying to communicate with it and that you want what you're asking for.

Since everyone is different, I recommend you experiment with the process until you find what works best for you. This leads us to the final step in the process.

Step 6 - Take action!

Except for very rare occasions, this isn't going to be a magic wishing-well effect. You're not going to be able to just say, "I want this," then go blithely along until it shows up on your couch. Like everything else in life, the more effort you put into pursuing what you want, the more likely you are to get it.

Part of the way the Law of Attraction works is by the activation of the reticular activating system, or RAS for short. What this nifty little brain structure does for you is:

- Respond to something novel - in other words, if you've never come across it before, the RAS will have a tendency to cause you to focus on it.

- Respond to something that affects your survival - from being able to instantly detect when someone says your name to seeing a car speeding toward you.

- Respond to something that's important to you - this is the bit that we're going to focus on in this process. This is what allows you to notice something that's related to what you're trying to manifest. It also has a direct impact on you when you're experiencing a case of cognitive dissonance.

Cognitive dissonance is, per Wikipedia®, "the mental stress or discomfort experienced by an individual who holds two or more contradictory beliefs, ideas, or values at the same time, or is confronted by new information that conflicts with existing beliefs, ideas, or values."

A perfect example of this is when you purchase a new car, you suddenly see a bunch of the same make and/or model of car on the street. It almost makes you feel like, just after you bought it, they had a huge sale and everyone went out and bought one as well. What's really happening is, before you bought the vehicle, you didn't really pay attention to what was on the road. When you bought the vehicle, however, you probably harbored some feelings that you might not have been making a good decision. This causes the RAS to jump into play and start letting you to notice all the other cars that match yours. This allows your subconscious mind to determine that, because a lot of other people are driving the same make and model, then it must have been a good decision. This allows you to dissipate the unconscious stress that was created by the initial purchase.

You might be wondering why I'm focusing on this so much. It's simple really. Once you've gone through steps 1-5, and you start taking action to achieve your desire, your RAS is going to start 'keeping an eye out' for situations that will help you progress toward your goal. It's also another reinforcing mechanism that tells your subconscious that you really want this, which in turn prods your mind to keep a look out for ways to bring it to you sooner.

My personal suspicion is that it also brings into play another process that most people aren't consciously aware of. Per Dr. Albert Mehrabian, author of Silent Messages, a whopping 93% of all communication is nonverbal. More specifically, body language makes up 55% of all communication between people. I firmly believe that people around you can pick up on those nonverbal cues to pass along your desires to the people who can help you achieve them. I also firmly believe that, since this communication is a two-way street, your subconscious is also picking up those nonverbal replies, subtly guiding you ever closer to your goal.

I honestly think that this process is where a lot of intuition and 'gut feelings' come from. Your RAS 'radar' picked up a signal telling your subconscious mind that, if you go here or do that or call so-and-so, you'll move closer to your goal

Even with all that, if you don't take action to pursue your desire, all these other 'coincidences' won't have the opportunity to take place. Now that you have the basics down, we'll move on to the next chapter, how to improve your results.

CHAPTER 3

METHODS OF IMPROVING RESULTS

As mentioned several times already, but bears repeating, is that the mechanisms that let the Law of Attraction work reside in the subconscious and unconscious mind. The better your subconscious mind understands what you're trying to accomplish, the better it's going to be at manifesting it. With that understanding, it only makes sense to learn techniques that allow you to more directly access those regions of the mind.

In order to understand how all these techniques work, you need to have a basic understanding of how your mind works and how your different brain states affect it. The most important thing to understand is the different brain-wave frequencies your brain operates at, namely, the Alpha and Theta brain-wave states.

Physical techniques

While I'm not going to go into any great depth about all the benefits learning how to reach these altered brain-wave states create, I am going to give a very basic overview of how it can help you in your quest to manifest stuff. If you're curious about the topic though, I've added a couple books to the further reading list at the end of this book.

Alpha brain-wave state

The primary brain-wave pattern we want to focus on is the Alpha state. This is the state you enter when you become deeply relaxed, like just before you drift off to sleep. The reason this state is important is that it's the first one that allows you a more direct, almost unfiltered, access to your subconscious mind. It's also the state where your creativity starts opening up, your memory improves, and your ability to learn new information increases due to the lack of filters your subconscious mind normally has in place when you're fully conscious.

Taking a step back, the thing to realize is, when you're fully awake, your subconscious mind uses filters to categorize and restrict the amount of information you're consciously aware of. It keeps your conscious mind from becoming overwhelmed by too much information. For example, when you're walking down the sidewalk, you don't normally pay attention to traffic going by. As far as your subconscious mind is concerned, the traffic isn't important enough to notice consciously. If a car locked up its breaks, however, your subconscious mind would pass that sound to your conscious mind since your survival might be threatened.

It's these same filters that makes it hard to transmit your affirmations and desires back down to your subconscious mind. But when you drop down to the Alpha level, you remove most of those filters, allowing you to directly access your subconscious mind.

Honestly, this is really as deep as you need to go in order to improve your results. It's the easiest level to reach, easiest level to stay mentally aware (the deeper you go, the more likely you are to fall asleep), and it's the easiest to learn. Going deeper into the Theta level isn't needed, but because it's closely related to the Alpha level, I'm going to briefly discuss it for those who are interested and/or who get recordings that push you that deep.

Theta brain-wave state

The Theta level is a slower frequency than Alpha level. For our purposes, it's important to understand that this level is associated with enhanced creativity and where the mind pulls together random bits of info and link them together in unexpected ways. Why this is important is that, not only does it enhance your mind's creative problem solving ability (needed for trying to figure out different ways to help you manifest your desire), it also allows you to filter and cross-reference what you know and create solutions from material you conscious mind would consider random information.

That second part is someone difficult to describe, but I'll give it a shot. Say you're trying to get introduced to "Important client A." In your research, you find out that they have a dog. Not too surprising or remarkable. Now say you have a friend that also has a dog. Again, not that special. Now, what if your friend got in the mail a coupon to bring their dog in for a free shampoo and trim on a specific day of the week.

With that situation, your unconscious mind might make the link between the coupon for free dog grooming and the possibility that "Important client A," might have receive the same coupon. It might have also decided that you should find a way to tag along with your friend, assuming they decided to take advantage of the special offer. Or maybe your friend can't take their dog because of prior commitments, but you offer to take their dog because they watched your kid recently, or something similar. All these coincidences add up to you being at the groomer at the same time as the client you've been trying to contact.

While this is a completely fabricated scenario, stranger things have happened. Being able to reach the Theta state can give this type of process a boost. It might also strengthen the tendency for you to solve problems while you're sleeping, since you bounce between Theta and Delta levels, Delta being the level Carl Jung theorized was the level someone could connect with the collective unconscious. If it exists, being able to tap into that can definitely help you manifest your desires. Since it's supposed to be the place where we, as a civilization, share our collective memories, the possibility to inject your request into it might help tremendously. Worst case scenario, you become well rested. What have you got to lose?

Eye position

This is one of those little things that can help out significantly when it comes to accessing the Alpha state. Researchers aren't really sure why, but just by lifting your gaze approximately 20 degrees, you start generating more Alpha brain-waves. With this bit of knowledge, when you start trying to descend to the Alpha level, just changing your point of attention higher can help significantly.

For example, start by sitting in a chair approximately ten feet away from the wall. If you were to stare straight ahead, your line of sight would be at 0 degrees. By shifting your gaze up to a point approximately one foot higher, then your gaze would be approximately 20 degrees higher. This is the point of gaze you want to aim for when trying to induce more Alpha brain-waves. Don't get too hung up on this though. It's better to lift your gaze slightly higher than to be slightly too low.

Meditation

Meditation is a great way to still your mind, clear stray thoughts, and easily slip into the Alpha state. One thing to keep in mind is, you're going to slightly change the actual process most forms of meditation recommend.

For most forms of meditation, the main intention is to focus your thoughts down to either a blank slate or one single thought/idea/ concept. Where you're going to modify it is, instead of that one individual thought/concept, you instead focus on your visualization/affirmation.

With that simple modification, you turn a good mental fitness program into a laser-targeted method to manifest your desire. Unfortunately, there's no way I can provide an all-encompassing review of all the forms of meditation out there. I'll leave it to you to discover the one that's right for you. To get you started, I've recommended a book in the further reading section at the end of this book.

Silva method

This program, in my opinion, is probably one of the best available for manifesting things. It seems tailor-made to take advantage of the Law of Attraction. Even though they never come right out and say it, a lot of what the system talks about seems either directly or indirectly related to the Law of Attraction and manifesting what you desire.

I'll give a basic overview of the process here, but there's a lot of material available in that program that seems to be custom made for manifesting stuff, like how to visualize changes in your life, how to have situations and things appear physically in your life, etc. I can't recommend this program enough. The book itself is, The Silva Mind Control Method, by Jose Silva.

The basic process for learning and using the Silva method begins by practicing it when you first wake up since you're still in a mild Alpha brain-wave state. The process is:

1. Upon awakening, go to the bathroom, then crawl back in bed.

2. Set your alarm for 15 minutes in case you fall back asleep (very easy to do in the beginning until you're used to functioning in the Alpha state).

3. Close your eyes, lift your gaze up to between 20 - 45 degrees above the position your eyes are in when looking straight ahead and relax.

4. Starting from 50, slowly count backward, mentally giving yourself the command to relax, until you reach 1.

5. After a few tries, sometimes even on the first attempt, you should be at the Alpha level.

6.   Remain at this level for around 10 minutes, then bring yourself back out of this state by counting from 1-5, giving yourself affirmations that when you 5, you'll become more alert, awake, and feeling better and more energized.

Once you get used to reaching the basic level of skill, meaning you consistently reach the Alpha level, you can start adding in your visualizations for manifesting. A thing to note is that there's a specific process for adding these visualizations into your Silva-based meditation.

The way to add your visualizations is:

1.   Once you reach the Alpha level, start visualizing your life as it currently is, in reference to what you want to manifest. For example, if you want people to treat you better at work, you'd start this process by visualizing what a typical day at your job would be like. You don't want it to be too vibrant or have much emotional energy invested in the current, 'bad' image.

2.   The next step would be bringing in the visualization of what you want from the left side of your 'field of vision,' pushing the current visualization off the right edge of your 'field of vision.'

3.   Once the desired visualization is up on your mental 'screen,' you'll want to bask it in for a few minutes, investing as much emotional energy into it. Imagine what it would feel like, smell like, and sound like if you had already received or reached what you desired and were currently enjoying it.

4. After a short time, you'd blank out the image, the bring up the image of your current situation again before progressing through steps 2-3 again.

5. Repeat this process a few more times, until you start losing focus or energy.

6. Bring yourself out of your Alpha state and continue on with your day.

Technological assistance

Since the whole idea of improving your manifestation skills revolves around reaching the Alpha level, and in some cases Theta, then it makes sense that any method that can get you to that level would be a good idea.

Surprisingly enough, there's a real easy way to reach the Alpha level with very little practice. There's an audio technology out there that can literally force your brain to drop down to the Alpha and Theta levels without any effort on your part other than relaxing and listening to them with a headset. What I'm talking about is something called binaural beat recordings.

Granted, you're going to have to do some research into this topic on your own. Unfortunately, some people react unfavorably when exposed to this technology. Unless you're ready for it, this technology can sometimes dredge up emotional 'stuff' that you've mentally buried over time, things that you might not be prepared to deal with. While this type of reaction is uncommon, it's not impossible. With that said, most people experience great results from using these types of audio recordings for self-improvement. In this respect, the technology is pretty mature.

Something to keep in mind is, we'll almost be using these recordings 'off label' for lack of a better way of describing it. These recordings are crafted for self-improvement specifically, but we're only interested in their ability to force us to enter the Alpha and/or Theta levels. so we're not quite using them for their intended purpose. With that said, what you're looking for is recordings that are just audio tracks. You don't want any type of vocal component, whether audible or subliminal. Any vocal component can adversely affect your actual manifestation process.

Once you find the recording that works best for you and your purposes, then the magic can really happen. Within minutes of starting to listen, no matter how stressed you are, regardless of everything you have running through your mind, you'll effortlessly start dropping into the Alpha and/or Theta level. Once there, it's just a matter of working on your affirmations and visualizations until the recording ends. It's that simple.

CHAPTER 4

POSSIBLE PROBLEMS AND SOLUTIONS

With all that we've covered, and all the techniques I've suggested, you'd wonder why everyone isn't doing this and getting everything they want. It just seems too simple and easy to work as described.

Unfortunately, even though theoretically it is this simple, there's a lot that can keep it from working. More specifically, working the way we want it to or as rapidly as we'd like. The problem is, when it comes to manifesting, we're our own worst enemy.

Since the Law of Attraction takes place in the unconscious mind, we have no real control over the process. Sure, we can go through the motions, and with the material covered, improve on the results. Unfortunately, there's always the chance that, buried somewhere in your unconscious, you have some form of block to what you're trying to manifest.

As touched on in chapter 3, money is usually high on the list of areas that people have formed mental blocks for. What I hope to provide in this chapter is a few methods to try and clear out these mental blocks, allowing you to remove resistance to your desires.

While I'm not a doctor, and in that aspect I highly recommend talking to a professional if you think you do have some of these deep seated beliefs, some of this material has helped numerous people clear out mental blockages. Again, we'll be using this material slightly outside of what it was designed for. Then again,

I really can't think of any techniques that were developed specifically for practicing the Law of Attraction, but one of the ones I go over comes close. Unlike the audio technology mentioned previously, we'll be using them closer to their original purpose.

Clearing out your mental junk

The tools we're going to be talking about were designed to help you clear out your mental junk without causing huge mental or emotional upheavals. One method was designed to help you address your issues in a very general, but very effective, way. The other one actually was more geared toward clearing your inner mind to allow the universal energy that powers the Law of Attraction to flow to you. Both techniques are very simple, on the surface, to perform. Once you understand and experience what they can do, however, you come to the realization that they are actually working at very deep levels of your psyche. Also, both methods will require you to take ownership of your issues at some level. With that said, let's get started.

Sedona Method

The basic process is:

1. Focus on the issue or situation you want to feel better about

2. Ask yourself, "Could I let this feeling go?"

3. Next, ask yourself, "Would I?"

4. Finally, ask yourself, "When?"

That is the Sedona method, in its entirety... Really. At face value, it seems too simple to work, but like most things in this area, the simple tools have the biggest impact on your life.

This whole process has one goal in mind. To allow you to acknowledge your situation as it really is. Until that happens, until you take ownership of the issue, you'll never be able to make progress. The problem will always be 'out there.' As long as it's 'out there,' we unconsciously give ourselves permission to believe we have no control over it, that it's outside of our ability to affect. Basically, it's a 'victim' mentality.

But once we take ownership of it, we tell our inner mind that we accept that, either directly or indirectly, we're the reason we're in our current situation, that we somehow caused it. By taking ownership of it, we tell ourselves that we do have the power to change the situation, that we have direct control over it. Once we do that, it's only a matter of determining what has to be done to progress in the direction we choose.

This process also gives us the mental space to accept the situation as it really is, not how we believe it to be. Have you ever seen someone that, no matter how much evidence to the contrary, goes blithely along, refusing to accept the situation? A perfect example of this are hoarders. To everyone else, the hoarder just has loads of garbage surrounding them. To the hoarder, everything is valuable. They refuse to look at the reality of the situation, that they're living in an environment that's bad for them. The whole point of therapy for them is to face the reality of the situation.

Once you've recognized what you want to change and have given yourself permission to accept the situation, you give yourself the option to let it go. There's no wrong answer here. If you're not ready to let go of it yet, that's fine. The important thing is to let yourself realize that it is, in fact, a choice you can make. That you can choose to let go of the feelings for your ex, or hang on to them for a while longer. Either answer is fine. What you'll find though is, by actually facing the issue head on and giving yourself permission to move past it, regardless of your answer, you'll actually start to move beyond it.

Which brings us to the final part... asking yourself, "When will I be willing to let go of the feeling/situation." For most people, the answer is, "NOW." For others, the answer is, "not quite yet." What's really cool about this final step is, once you answer the question, a lot of times, you'll actually experience a physical sensation. Now everyone is different, and you might not experience what someone else might. What I can tell you is, something will happen once your unconscious mind realizes you're serious about this process.

For me, the general process feels similar to the sensation you get when you get a cold chill, but without the shivering. It's just a mild tingling throughout my chest and abdomen. But it can also be so much more. The one situation that sticks out firmly in my mind happened a few years ago during hurricane Sandy. At the time, I worked in a call center for a large company. Because of all the damage sustained, we were being forced to work fifteen hours straight, six days a week. This went on for several weeks.

Unfortunately, I have a back injury that I acquired in the military, one serious enough that I collect disability for. Being forced to sit in an office chair for that many hours a day, for that many weeks, wreaked havoc on my lower spine. Because of the pain, for nearly a year after that situation, I had ongoing daily pain that frequently flared up enough that I missed days of work at a time, several times a month. Missing all that work seriously impacted our income during that time.

Why I bring this all up is, I developed a good dose of anger and resentment toward the company because I felt that they were the reason I was suffering so much. One day I finally realized that the company didn't really cause the issue... the severe pain in my back. It was due to a force of nature that nobody had any control over. Once I came to that realization, I went through the Sedona method. When I asked myself if I was ready and willing to let go of the anger and resentment, I told myself I was. When I asked myself, "when," and replied, "now," a funny thing happened. I immediately felt all the muscles in my lower back, the same muscles that had been tight for nearly a year, loosen up and relax. Within five minutes of going through this process and letting go of negative feelings I'd been carrying for the same amount of time, I was nearly pain free. By the end of the shift, my back had completely relaxed and had audibly, and loudly, popped back into position.

Looking back on it, I carried around all that anger and resentment which in turn settled into my lower back as pain. As soon as I told my inner self I was done with it, it let the tension go. Now while I can't promise that level of release, by consistently going through this process, you'll eventually clear out the blocks that are keeping you from your heart's desires. And just in case you need more proof, Jack Canfield, of Chicken Soup for the Soul fame and one of the stars from The Secret actually wrote the forward for the book.

Ho'oponopono

This method was made popular, maybe better known would be more accurate, by Joe Vitale, another star of The Secret, in his book, Zero Limits. In a nutshell, what Joe describes as

Ho'oponopono is based off the teachings of Ihaleakala Hew Len. Dr. Hew Len Worked at the Hawaii State Hospital for three years where they kept the criminally insane.

What makes where he worked interesting was, before Dr. Hew Len worked there, there was a high attrition rate and most of the inmates were never expected to see the light of day again. When Dr. Hew Len started working at the facility, his one condition was that he wouldn't be required to see the patients, let alone counsel them in person. Instead, he would review their files and then start using his clearing method, which is based off of being 100% responsible for anything that showed up in his life. Put another way, his belief was that the reason these people were insane was due to something within himself causing it. He felt that, since he was there experiencing their insanity, then their illness was a reflection of what was within himself.

With that belief, he would proceed to clear himself of this problem by turning the issue over to the divine by repeating to himself:

I love you
I'm sorry
Please forgive me
Thank you

From that process alone, within a few months, absenteeism went down, patients were being medicated less, and inmates were becoming well enough to be release.

With that type of ability to clear out blockages and unconscious programming, it only stands to reason that it could be of great value to you in your journey to clear out your unconscious programming, allowing you to manifest what you desire.

CHAPTER 5

CONCLUSION

So here we are at the end of our short journey. Hopefully you've gained some valuable information from this short book that helps you manifest the life you want to have. The tools I've provided to boost your manifestation abilities, along with the ones to break down any mental walls or blocks, should propel you on your way forward into the life you were meant to live.

None of these tools are hard to use or implement, but because they ARE so simple, it's easy to disregard them or have the mistaken belief that they won't work. While I won't promise that it'll always work every time, or that it'll happen instantly, I will promise you that these tools will change your life if you give them the chance to.

Just try to practice them consistently for three months. Most experts will tell you that it only takes a month to develop a habit, and there's a lot of evidence for it, but the Law of Attraction and manifesting is different. It's not just a matter of developing a habit. It's a journey of developing a belief, of having faith, in something more than yourself. It's understanding that if you'll only let it happen, the creator will provide you everything you ask for. Live in light.

"Ask and it will be given to you; seek and you shall find; knock and the door will be opened to you. For everyone who asks receives; the one who seeks finds; and the one who knocks, the door will be opened." Matthew 7:7-8

Oh... And before you go...

If you've received any value from this book, could you do me a favor and leave a review at the Kindle website for me? The way other people find books of value is by how many reviews the book gets. More reviews also increase exposure of the book to other readers because Amazon promotes it more. It'll only take a few minutes of your time and it could very well help someone else change their life because they trusted you.

Please leave a review on Amazon for me.

Also, you can visit me on the web at:

www.TheAttractiveLife.com

Thank you again for purchasing my book and may the light of the creator shine down on you.

APPENDIX A

Further reading

Below is just a quick sampling of books that can help you in your quest to manifest your desires.

- Byrne, Rhonda. The Secret. Atria Books and Beyond Words Publishing, 2006

- Dwoskin, Hale. The Sedona Method. Sedona Press, 2003

- Harris, Bill. Thresholds of the Mind. Centerpointe Press, 2007

- LeShan, Lawrence. How to Meditate. Bantam, 1974

- Silva, José. The Silva Mind Control Method. Pocket Books, 1977

- Vitale, Joe. Attractor Factor. Wiley, 2008

- Vitale, Joe. The Key. Wiley, 2008

- Vitale, Joe. Zero Limits. Wiley, 2007